About the Author

The complexity of family is something we all have to find our way through, but keep to yourself and surround yourself with those who give you strength when it is needed most. Find your people and go with them, family is more than blood.

Life is Full of Moments

Trisha Doherty

Life is Full of Moments

Vanguard Press

VANGUARD PAPERBACK

© Copyright 2024
Trisha Doherty

The right of Trisha Doherty to be identified as author of this work has been asserted by her in accordance with the Copyright, Designs and Patents Act 1988.

All Rights Reserved

No reproduction, copy or transmission of this publication may be made without written permission.
No paragraph of this publication may be reproduced, copied or transmitted save with the written permission of the publisher, or in accordance with the provisions of the Copyright Act 1956 (as amended).

Any person who commits any unauthorised act in relation to this publication may be liable to criminal prosecution and civil claims for damages.

A CIP catalogue record for this title is available from the British Library.

ISBN 978 1 80016 862 6

This is a work of fiction. Names, characters, businesses, places, events and incidents are either the product of the author's imagination or used in a fictitious manner. Any resemblance to actual persons, living or dead, or actual events is purely coincidental.

Vanguard Press is an imprint of
Pegasus Elliot Mackenzie Publishers Ltd.
www.pegasuspublishers.com

First Published in 2024

Vanguard Press
Sheraton House Castle Park
Cambridge England

Printed & Bound in Great Britain

To my rock, JD. Without you I would not have been able to accomplish this. We have had an adventure and will have many more to come.

Acknowledgements

To my three children, my husband, and to Mum with love

Feeling Empty

My head is numb
I don't feel anything
Am I awake?
Am I asleep?
My consciousness is in no man's land, no thoughts presenting
Do I cut myself to feel
Or do I give into the numbness and just sleep till the feeling wears off?
Another opportunity squandered
Why do I set myself expectations?
I am bound to fail
I am bound to fall
I am empty
I am depleted
Is it worth trying?
Is it worth waking up from this stupor?
I need to wake up
I need to be positive
I am strong
I will not be beaten.

Smile Upon Your Face

Satisfying days come and go
The memories put a smile on your face
A walk to your local café
A walk in the autumn sun
These are some of my favourite things
The conversation, the laughter without needing to speak
The company is warm and understanding
The air that fills your senses, the good smells the bad smells
Snuggle under a dooner on an autumn day to warm your bones
Letting the animals sit on you, or next to you
Being in the moment
These are some of my favourite things.

Sundays

Sundays are the best and the worst
No alarms on a Sunday
Chill out, watch a movie, read a book.
Try not to think on a Sunday
Let the small things entertain you.
Go for a stroll, or a drive on a Sunday.
The St Kilda Esplanade on a Sunday.
Sundays are for exploring,
For winding down.
Don't let the worries of the world take you away.
Don't rush on a Sunday; it will be gone in the blink of
    an eye.
Soon it will be dinner time, get ready for work time
To face the world
Leave that for Monday.
Enjoy that one last breath on a Sunday.

Insanity

What is the definition of insanity?
Is it believing what we are told without question
Or is it questioning what we are being told?
The lack of humanity is everywhere, cannot see a smile
You look up, they look down
No break from this dystopian existence
Do we listen to our governance or do we listen to ourselves?
What if everyone broke from these chains tomorrow, would that be insane?
Am I insane for wanting to live and plainly exist?
Am I insane for thinking of ways to sleep forever, or am I sane for wanting this to end?
Am I insane for wanting to connect with my family,
Or go to my favourite coffee shop?
Can you differentiate between the sane and the insane?

But a Number

What is age but a number?
Do we learn with age or is it too late?
What if we aged backwards, would we adapt sooner?
Is your age a reflection of your wisdom?
What is too young?
What is too old, where did these ideas come from?
Why does our age dictate our dress or participation in life?
Age is but a number
Where has the time gone you ask,
You try to remember
One day into the next
One year into the next
With each passing year comes new experiences
Your age doesn't define you
Age is but a number.

Thankful

On days that are a struggle
Be thankful for
Something - anything
Be thankful for those that you can turn to
Be thankful for the sunshine that helps the smallest of
    flowers to grow
Be thankful for those who have simply believed in you
Or simply acknowledge your individuality
Be thankful for those that make you laugh
Be thankful for the day
Be thankful for the smell of a hot cup of coffee
Thank yourself for trying
For seeing the best when the worst is in your thoughts
For seeing that you matter and have an abundance to
    offer
Be thankful for one small thing today.

Celebrate Your Individuality

Celebrate yourself
Celebrate you are still living
Age is just a number
You've been made to feel ashamed
You've felt you can't do anything right
You feel like you're always stepping on toes
You feel like you're in the way
You feel dejected
You are still here
You saw the sun rise another day
If you feel no one is kind to you, be kind to yourself
Forgive yourself
Only you know you
If you've been called a snob because you weren't full of greeting when you walked into work
If you've been called weird because you don't fit the mould
Align with those that see you
In a world where everyone wants you to fit into a box, fit into a circle
Be you and you will be a magnet for others
Don't hide yourself away

Don't try to fit in at the cost of your individuality
Be you
There is only one of you
Be kind to yourself
Respect yourself
You will sparkle and shimmer, and like-minded people will sparkle with you.

Celebrate your Individuality (cont.)

You have made it this far
One day at a time
Let the sun keep shining on your face one morning at a time
Be you
Live life your way
Direct your energy to things that give you positivity
Be you and don't shy away
Be you and embrace it
Leave the nay-sayers behind
Be your individual self for all time
Celebrate your individuality.

Cannot Control All Things

I cannot control what I cannot control
I can manage my inner dialogue
I cannot control the weather
I can prepare for it
I cannot control the traffic
I can take precautions
I cannot control the way people speak to me
I can choose how I react, and to walk away
I cannot control people's attitudes toward me
I can be respectful
I can lower my expectations of others so as to not get disappointed
I can come to learn that not everyone I come into contact with is my friend
I can manage my attitude
I can manage my inner thoughts
I can take a breath
I can take a moment to process
I can be kind to others
Life is an adventure
Adventures cannot be controlled
Adventures are wilful

Adventures are for learning
I cannot control all that is around me
I can learn from my experiences.

Effort and Energy

Why do I strain?
The effort is not reciprocated
Kindness forgotten
It's taking a toll on my being
Yet I'm trying not to re-do past mistakes
Live past regrets
I'm trying
No one is noticing
What is $1 worth in this world?
Why am I not worth more than this?
I seek no glory
I seek no praise
Acknowledge my effort and I will repay tenfold
Show me the way and I will follow
Tell me the way and I will listen
Recognise my diligence and I will be OK
Rewards I do not seek
If I am there tomorrow, appreciate my valuable time in your service
Walk with me and we will be journeymen
Learn to understand me and I will be forever loyal
My effort and time are to be cherished

My effort and time are valuable
A commodity I am not
A being of worth I am
Treat me so, and I will show you my value and my worth.

Different Language

We are talking to each other
I don't understand you
You don't understand me
Why don't you ask me questions?
I don't know what I'm supposed to say
My head is swirling
You've misconstrued my words
My words are direct
My words are simple
No hidden meanings
So why do we not understand each other?
I'm exhausted, having to wrestle this out
Untangle myself from misinterpreted dialogue
I am who I am
I make no apology
Let's be civil
Let's keep it simple
Let's meet in the middle and figure it out
I am confused by your demeanour
Your interpretation of my words leaves me paralysed
    with emotion
I have no inference

If I say it and you do not understand
Please ask
Ask me until we figure it out
Ask me to determine, to clarify.

Different Language (cont.)

Ask me and I will tell you
Nothing hidden
Nothing sinister in my words
I am not melodic
I am pointed
Why beat around the bush and play guessing games with each other?
Let's put it behind us
Let's move on from this confusion
Let us be clear
Let us be simple
In times of misunderstandings, let us seek clarity
Let's not be accusatory
Keep it honest
Keep it simple
No menace behind my words
Let us learn to speak the same language
Let us start again.

Promises

Promises are made
Inclusivity is promised
Open dialogue between all encouraged
Reality is not what is promised
Inclusivity not delivered for the neurodiverse
Open dialogue misunderstood
Promises of supportive environment not yielded as yet
Promises are not meant to be broken
How do I feel comfortable if I am not supported?
I am coming across as difficult
Emotionally unstable
I am embarrassed
I need to stay
I am strong, I will overcome these obstacles
I am not comfortable I was promised I would be
Not everyone is my friend
Not everyone is my confidante
Fifty years on and I need to remind myself of these things
Those that need to know my ins and outs are my friends
My confidantes
Do not promise what you cannot deliver

It is disingenuous
It sets up for false confidence in an unfamiliar environment
I am told I need to stay
Accept things how they are.

Promises (cont.)

Accept me for me
Accept my promises will be true
I will meet your expectations and more
Courtesy and acceptance in your world are all I ask
Do not promise what you cannot deliver
Promise within reason and I will stand by your side.

Inner Thoughts

Everyone says stick it out
Your strong
It will blow over
How do I stop thinking the worst?
How do I stop caring about what others think?
How do I redirect my thinking?
My animals give me comfort
They bring me peace, how do I capture that in every moment?
Hold onto it
Harness it for my renewed focus
I can't stop thinking of the negative
Over and over the record in my head playing repetitively
I need it to stop
I eat comfort food that helps for a short while
I need to stop dwelling on events that have passed
Focus on the present
I need to be numb for a moment
I need to reset
I need to get out of my head
I need to refocus

Find new strategies
Contemplate the positive
Not everything is within my control
Accept me.

Inner Thoughts (cont.)

Accept my thoughts
Refocus
And through this I will be able to climb mountains
I need to love me
Accept I am not everyone's cup of tea
One day at a time
One hour at a time
One minute at a time
It is but a moment in time.

There Once Was a Party

There once was a party
The whole world was invited
Not me
I was not invited
As I did not follow the rules
"The rules of what?" I asked
The way you're supposed to behave
I did not dress like the others
You cannot wear bright green shoes with rainbows in
    your later years
You do not speak like the rest of us
"What do you mean?" I asked
Well that's exactly what we mean, you have to ask
You are unsure of your words
I said, "OK
I will have a party on my own
Where I can dress how I want
Speak how I want
Have all the colours of the rainbow on my food."
They looked at me and asked, "Why?"
I said, "Because then I can dance like no one is watching
And I will be free

I will not have to fit into a mould of any kind
They said that sounds like fun."
"Can we join your party?"
I said, "Absolutely, as long as you promise to dance like no one is watching."

Guardian Angel

My guardian angel
I feel you watching over me
I feel you keeping me safe
I know when my tears fall you catch them
When I smile you smile with me
I see you through my animals and their unquestionable
 trust and love for me
I see it in the stars above me
My guardian angel looking down on me whispers, "You
 are not alone."
The signs are there that you are on my side
You help me to see the sun when the days are dark
You help me to see kindness when I am looking through
 the fog
My guardian angel, you bring me peace when confusion
 is surrounding me
I feel your arms protecting me
You will not let me dwell in sadness
I know that my guardian angel is always close by
My guardian angel is by my side and puts their arms
 around me when the tears swell in my eyes
You have always been with me, will always be with me
Never taken for granted my guardian angel.

Replay in My Head

I am alone in the dark
The replay goes over and over in my mind
What did I say?
How did I say it?
Why was I scolded?
I try to rationalise
Come to terms
What's done is done
Cannot go back in time
What would I say, would it change?
Or would the events be the same?
Will people look at me strangely tomorrow?
Am I the talk of the town?
I hope not
I want to be a quiet mouse
Why can't I just let things be?
Why can't I understand what's in front of me?
How did this occur?
How did this escalate?
I was doing so well
I'm exhausted

I need to sleep, but the record player in my head is on
    repeat
Action by action
Word by word, it's stuck there.

Replay in My Head (cont.)

How do I make it stop?
My eyes are droopy
My anxiety heightened
I don't want any more confrontations
Let me be
Let me be me
Let me go back to being a quiet little mouse.

I Look Like You

I look like you
I stand like you
I move like you
But I am not like you
I react slower
I move with caution
My energy is waning before I start the day
My connection to what is happening around me is slower
My brain tells me to take it easy, but I want to fit in
So I jump in
The fire in my legs doesn't dissipate
My head, pounding, hasn't stopped since I woke up
I'm confused, what did you say?
I won't ask you to repeat cause I'll figure it out
I can't stop thinking about the end of the day
Need my comfort
My bed
My animals
Tears about to stream down my face
I am not the same as you
Minute by minute the day will pass by
I will end up in my comfort with no expectations
I will do better tomorrow with being more like you.

Too Much

It's too peopley out there
In the big wide world
Too much noise
I may bump into someone I know
Chit chat required
My thoughts escape me
I don't recognise you today
I may tomorrow
My head needs quiet, so I look down not up
Don't want to leave my house for a while
Out there is unknown
Unexpected
Confusion
It's so bright I need my sunglasses
Too much going on
I need to get dressed
I can't decide
It's too peopley outside, I'll stay inside for a little longer

Slipping Away
To my mum

You are slipping away minute by minute
You are saying your goodbyes
You are at peace with your weightlessness
You have not had a boring life
You know that the deep sleep awaits you
The light is leaving your eyes
The humour shines every so faintly
You will live in your grandkids' hearts
Your stories will be told forever more
To have one more conversation
One more moment
One more Moscato
You have had a heavy burden on your shoulders
Your faith has seen you through
You have held your head high when others would have given up
We have had conflict
We have had moments of togetherness
Forgiveness gave us peace
Your eyes are becoming heavy
This world is slipping from your grip

You will be a great grandmother for the second time
You are ready for a long rest now
You are one of a kind
You will be missed
Be at peace.

New Beginnings

The news of new life
Anticipation
Excitement
No expectations
No limitations
The future is unwritten
Not uncertain
Ready to love another unconditionally
Ready to give without expectation
The gender is of no concern
The unborn is ready to be nurtured by all who surround
    you
Legacies to be passed on
Stories to be told
Adventures to be had
Memories to be created
Can't wait to see your face
You are precious even though you are unaware
You will be loved, you are loved.

Frozen

My brain is stuck
It's frozen
Doesn't want to listen to the alarm day by day
I fight past it, but in the end, sleep draws me in
My body stuck in mud
Nowhere to run, nowhere to move
Time passes, I cannot get out of this hole
I need to change something up
I need to get out of this
My brain is tired
It doesn't want to think
It just wants to be
To create, to run wild
It feeds the information to the rest of me
The rest of me follows
I need to rest
But along the way I have enjoyed the journey
I can only get past my toes
My brain does not let me go any further
My brain panics and stops me from taking chances
My brain stops believing in me and what I am capable
    of

My brain is frozen and does not want me to carry on
Two parts of me fighting, the conflict is exhausting
I cannot let my brain win this time.

Time

Time is but a moment
Time is but the hands on a clock
It is what you do with that time that matters
Do you spend it with loved ones?
Do you take adventures?
Do you take care of yourself?
Time is but a moment
A short passage of your life
A meaningful interaction
Or a distraction to fill the gap
Everything we do is based on time
Time to get up
Time to go to bed
Time to do things in between
Time helps us capture the memory
We do not have to let the clock run our lives
The clock is our reminder that we cannot get moments back
We cannot rewind
We cannot redo
Be careful with your time
Treasure the time you have and spend it well
Use this precious time to create memories and moments
To fill the rest of time with precious stories.

Kindness

It is strange when you are used to indifference
When kindness walks your way
Shows its face
Kindness is not an action I am used to
I do not know how to respond or react
I like being kind and giving without expectation
I am unused to strangers being kind in turn
It is a weird feeling to appreciate someone else's effort
To be recognised for your contribution
To be understood when you have failed before
Instead of being scolded you are being complimented
Your worth is seen and valued
How do I manage this feeling, will it be fleeting or ongoing?
Will I continue to be supported?
Doubts burn strong of my competence
How did I manage to gain their confidence?
A wave, a smile, these are all manageable acts of kindness
Expectations are now set upon me to repay the kindness
To concrete those beliefs falls upon me

Kindness and compliments placed upon me are difficult to place
Difficult to manage and difficult to respond to
But kindness is a true measure of gratitude and belief
True kindness comes without response
Without proof or justification, and is never equal it is given freely
When kindness is given, it lifts one's spirit.

Forethought

To live in the present
To not think about what might be tomorrow
To not think about future plans that have not come to fruition
To be present in all interactions
To accept the moment, to sit quietly
To not let my thoughts go roaming about what if
To not let my thoughts focus on how others see me
To just sit, to still my mind
To quiet the chatter in my head
Not to think about the past
Not to think about tomorrow
Be present, be in the now
Be with the people you are with in that moment
Accept the quiet
Accept the still photo in your mind
Accept that time can stand still for a moment.

Trust

Trust is something earned
Something treasured
As precious as any gold or silver
Once broken, cannot be given wholly
Like a broken vase, it will always feel different
Your being depends on it
Your soul thrives on it
Your life is in its hands
It is a simple thing
But so easily taken for granted
Trust is so much more than fidelity
It's a way of communication
It's a bond
It's understanding each other
Allowing the other to speak without judgement or insinuation
Taking each other at face value,
Respecting each other
Holding each other without prompting
Being honest without insult
Knowing you can count on each other
Knowing you are safe from the world around you
Trust is beautiful
Wear it proudly as it never fades.

Sleep Comes

The night-time stretches across your face
The angels beside you
Ready to take you into their arms
To take your tears
To take your fears
To cover you in a blanket of darkness
To allow you to rest your weary body
In the corners of your eyes, you know we are there
Watching over you
Guiding you down this path
You are not alone
The darkness is your warmth
Do not be afraid
The pain will be no more
Let sleep engulf you
Let it take you by the hand
You will be missed
Always loved
But go now, find your peace
Leave this world
Be free of your shackles
You will be in our hearts for always

Let sleep take you by the hand
Let sleep wrap you up in a soft cloud
Give in to the night as it welcomes you
Goodnight
Love you always.

Facing Death

When death is at your doorstep
Time moves slowly
The days into nights become longer and longer
The air stifling
But you welcome it for the peace it will bring
You grieve before it's time
You are anguished
You feel wronged
You also know it is time
The time is sad
Shared with loved ones
Death whispers in the night
The living ones pine and cherish their memories
Time stops to let you have one last look
As it starts up again it says, "Let go."
Death is not simple or pleasant
It is to be respected and accepted
Let it not rob you of your soul
Let it not shine despair on you for eternity
Let it be one door that closes behind you
Remember those in death in your heart for all time.

Goodnight

The sunlight burns my eyes
I can only see small stars in my eyes
Lingering teardrops that don't know how to fall
My head is heavy
My body is numb
To never hear your chatter again
To never see you smile again
To never see your unique style again
Reconciling what will never be again
A Moscato in your hand one more time would brighten my day
You have left this world
You are not forgotten
You have left lasting memories for us to recall
Your turmoil is put to rest
Your light will never go out, no matter the blackness of the sky
You remain always in our thoughts
In our reflections
In our likeness
As you say goodbye, a new generation enters who will hear your stories

And get to know you
To have had one more conversation with you is all I ask
I will just relive the ones we have had and play them over and over again
Goodnight to you
Sleep well my dear.

Take a Breath

When the world is moving fast around you
Stop, take a breath
Go take that trip
Go down that highway
Take in the moment
Don't compare yourself to others
Don't wish for something else to be
Live in that moment
Be happy in that minute
Be sad for those hours
Be angry for a second
But learn from those interactions, hold onto them
Don't let one moment pin you down
Move up
Move down
Take the next step
Take that leap
Start that project
Believe in you for a moment
Moments go by so quickly
Cannot relive, can only recall
How did you feel?

How did you fare?
Did you embrace it?
Take a deep breath and hold this moment
Moments turn into memories
Turn into stories
Turn into adventures
Be present
Be with those who encourage
Those that are like-minded
Willing to embrace the moment with you
Take a breath and I will take one with you.

Pets

My pets give me peace
They give me comfort
No need for words
We don't speak the same language
But we trust in each other
They rest on my lap
Nestle next to me
They bring calm to my inner storm
The snores
The deep breaths
The panting
The affection without question
The world is OK
A nice distraction
Positive focus providing care and nurture to each other
Surrounded by these three beings
Helps refocus
Provides comfort
Unquestionable trust
In good times, in sad times our pets are always there for us
Pets see us in a different light to our human companions

They are ready to greet us
Ready to accept us without question
Pets are a different kind of family.

Moving On

The days come and go
The sun rises
The sun sets
An event to attend
A game to play
Days turn into months
Months turn into years before we know it
We cannot stay static
We need to move
We need to play
We need to continue to connect with the living
We cannot be frozen in time
Stuck in the numbness
It doesn't bring you back, it only holds us back
We need to continue to cry when the moment takes us
We need to laugh again
Be joyous
Be brave
Be adventurous
Learn to live without the stabbing in our hearts
Treat every minute with importance
Treat others with kindness

Remember with respect
Don't forget to live today
Let sadness not overstay its welcome
Keep the memories close
But don't let them consume you
Take on the new
Be in the now
You have others that depend on you
Be strong
Wake up tomorrow and live again.

Born into a Car Crash

I was born in 1971. Not long before I was born, my family was involved in a serious car accident that would change theirs and my life forever in one moment.

My parents, grandmother and older two siblings were stationary on a highway due to a breakdown of the car, when a moving truck slammed into their vehicle, even though my dad tried to illuminate the vehicle with a torch.

In that one instant, that one single moment, I lost my grandmother and one of my siblings; and it changed my parents' and my life thereafter.

I was born the same year my eldest sibling died, in the same month she was born. I had rejection from my mother from birth, and my father as a child; no connection from that first moment of being born. It took me a very long time to understand or come to terms with the rejection from my mother, and a different process to acknowledge the rejection from my father.

Not to mention I was different from the others, and no one really explored how or why I was different; they just treated me differently, and/or corrected me for being inappropriate in actions or words.

One of the most vivid memories I have, and the one that still gives me nightmares no matter what my age, is this incident: I would have been around the age of six or seven. We were in a flat, and I remember hearing a lot of commotion. The door was slightly open, so I peeked and I saw my parents and a knife being wielded. I was horrified and I quickly went back to bed and tried not to remember.

When I brought it up years later, I always thought my dad had the knife against my mum, but it was my mum holding the knife, protecting my older sibling from my dad. No child should ever have to witness that, or anything similar it is one of the things that haunts my mind.

My parents divorced when I was eight years old; my dad was an alcoholic and not a nice one. Although he didn't physically abuse me, he did hurt my mum and verbally abused the rest of us. I recall the police visiting us in St Kilda a few times.

My mum remarried a little while later, to someone the polar opposite of herself, and who also carried severe emotional baggage. Where Mum could be the life of the party and enjoyed social gatherings, her second husband did not like the social aspects of life.

He cared for Mum in physical ways which she needed, right up until he passed. My children called him Granddad, as that is what he was to them. He was there when they were born, and even though he was different, he had affection for the grandchildren and was always willing to engage with them.

He died of bowel cancer, and as he disliked doctors and medical facilities, he refused to seek help even though he was in pain, and he never got it investigated until it was too late. From diagnosis to death was three months. My eldest was with me in his hospital room when he passed. Twelve months prior to his passing, my husband's father passed away. My husband's mother is still alive and very spritely for her age.

Mum could use emotional manipulation on us, whether it was deliberate or without understanding of what she was doing I will never know; so the trauma passed from the car accident to it impacting our lives on a daily basis.

It was later I learned that mum had acquired a brain injury from the accident, and I was told by other family members that she had changed. Again, I don't think people realised the impact that could have on a child, being told they were being raised by a stranger that was not familiar to those that were close to them.

Upon my reflection of my mum and the words of my children, I have come to learn that they felt cherished by her and saw her maternal instincts toward them. This makes me both happy and sad, knowing she had the capability, but maybe she did not have the tools to parent. Counselling was not offered automatically to those that suffered physical or emotional trauma for her generation. She suffered both: she lost her mum, the one person that may have helped her through those difficult circumstances.

When I was in grade six, I had a white singlet on, (never worn one since in public) and for whatever reason I lifted my arms and my mum picked me up and said very loudly, "You have hairs under your arm!" I was so embarrassed, but that was one example of how Mum could be.

I excelled in school, in all subjects except for maths, and Mum would get so cross, she just could not understand my difficulty with maths as she was quite good at it, but unless it was logical to me it didn't register.

The same was with literature; I could articulate my thoughts verbally but not on paper, yet I could mimic an accent in a book when reading out loud. My literature teacher was baffled, but it was left because I was getting by.

I learnt clarinet and was a decent player. I played in one high school band; however, I can only read music and not play by ear, unlike one of my siblings who could play several instruments and all by ear, along with sheets. Again, as I was able to do it fairly well so no one questioned my inability to understand music in other forms.

I was bullied in most schools I attended. I moved from one primary school due to the bullying, and it did not get any better in high school.

Being bullied at school and then going home to a different form of bullying, there never seemed to be any peace for a long time in my life. I think my saving grace was the community I was involved in; they were the ones for the most part that kept me sane and provided a distraction from the conflict surrounding me.

I would love to say the bullying stopped when I finished school, but I have been bullied as an adult in a variety of ways. The only thing I am thankful for is that social media was not around when I was in high school. My youngest was bullied not only in school, but also via social media; and so I have seen firsthand how bad that can be. Not to say my other children have not been bullied.

I went to eight primary schools, and four high schools (one of my own choosing); this is due to the number of times we moved house and area. The area I feel most connected to is St Kilda in Melbourne. I felt part of a community, I felt safe, and was not treated too differently at that stage of my life.

I was taught from a young age to believe in my views and to strongly uphold them. That has stayed with me until current times; but I also have learnt when not to go down that road, and how to read the room better.

I felt so alone for such a long time; even though at various times I had friends and did socialise, I never felt I belonged in any group or connected properly with friends. There was always a disconnect, and if anything went sideways, I somehow was the one to blame.

I ended up finding my way into office work, bookkeeping or accounts payable which are skills that I still use.

My husband and I met by chance in our late teens, and by our early-twenties we had our hands full with three children under three. I had a few medical issues with each birth, so we decided not to have any more.

Not long before we met, I attempted suicide where I ended up in hospital and was given charcoal to drink. My mum thought it was over a boy, but it actually wasn't; although I could not articulate what was inside my head at the time. I was referred to a therapist, and the only thing I got out of those sessions was to try to say no more often, which is still difficult for me to do.

My first child was delayed due to dilation issues, and my second was an emergency caesarean. They were placenta previa, and I still can see the bed filling with blood when the nurse placed the catheter in, and the only vision I had was of my mum running behind me; which is a fond memory in a weird way because it makes me laugh. My youngest was a dilation issue and induced after a while, like the first. The doctors were hesitant to induce due to having a caesarean with the previous birth.

During their infancy we were in and out of the Royal Children's Hospital a fair bit due to one of our children experiencing respiratory issues, to the point that while they were in hospital overnight, they were on their deathbed and my husband was called in and told the child might not survive the night. The child was given adrenalin and other medications, and not long after almost back to themselves.

They were diagnosed with random croup which was present in one in five children at the time and difficult to diagnose because it presents similar to asthma. We were in and out of hospital up until their early childhood. Unfortunately, this child always wanted to run around, and this is was one of the things that they could not be doing as it aggravates the symptoms. They also had a camera put down their throat to confirm it was nothing more serious because it seemed to linger longer than the normal time frame. It ended up being managed with steroid medication.

After our last child was born, I struggled to be myself. I couldn't hang out washing without feeling exhausted, I stopped cooking dinner on a regular basis, simple tasks would wear me out. This went on for a while, and so I started looking for information on what I was feeling, and one of the news programs did a story on M.E. Chronic Fatigue Syndrome. I made an appointment to see my GP with that information, and he validated my thoughts and sent me to a specialist which confirmed the diagnosis, along with ruling out other issues using blood tests.

I have now lived with M.E. Chronic Fatigue for over twenty years with no treatment, except for over-the-counter pain relief, and every now and then some whisky to help me sleep. My children have also grown up with me having this illness, and it is sad to say I was not the mother I wanted to be. I wanted to be so different to my own mother, so from an early age we got them into activities. Their first activity was Irish dancing and they were able to attend classes altogether.

The Irish dancing lessons put a spotlight on one of my children; the other two learnt so quickly and progressed as expected or quicker, however one struggled to get past a certain point even after several months, but we were never negative, always encouraging, and from there they all went to little athletics.

Two of my children did not have too many issues in primary school, but one did, either running late, or did not eat lunch, or could not keep their laces tied, and the homework drama. This child did several testings in primary school and there were issues, but nothing to suggest how to help them or what the primary cause was.

At times I would ask people to help out, either picking the children up or with meals, but there was always a negative underlying tone, and expectations that I would be required to meet, so we decided to move to a place where the children could walk to school. I really did not want to move them like I had to, but I also did not want them to miss too much school because of my ill health.

So, we moved across the bridge, where my husband moved the furthest away from his family at the time.

When I needed to work, I did; there are not many industries I have not dipped my hands in.

I applied to be a Teacher's Aide due to seeing the difficulties in one of my children, and I was pointed in the direction of Dr Richard Eisenmayer and got an appointment for a consultation. At the age of twelve, they were diagnosed as being autistic, which made so much more sense to us and them; however the school issues did not go away. The school just did not know how to work with them or how to assist them.

During their last years of school, we found a program that suited them to the point that they excelled in their classes and progressed to university.

I am proud of all my children, as they have been affected by my health and external factors that have influenced our lives.

In 2008/9 we lost everything. We had several investment properties and were struggling to deal with the situation, deciding how to move on and keep strong for the children.

We are a family of dog lovers, so no matter what else has taken place in our lives, us and the kids have had dogs to attend to, to distract them and give them unquestionable love and loyalty.

My father was not a better grandparent then a parent, which lead to me writing a letter to him, asking him to change his ways or we won't be part of his life.

He was toxic and he put his alcohol before any other important aspect of life; for example, even though he knew I was unwell and probably struggle to put dinner together when he would come and stay, instead of offering to assist in some capacity, the main component was having alcohol to drink.

I did not attend his funeral. Part of me feels bad and sad about this, and I had said to my husband a few times leading up to his departure that I should contact him, but this was also me all the time and I just was not sure what to say.

As complicated and difficult as my life has been with my mum, I have stayed around as much as possible, even to the point of forgiving her and coming to the realisation that she cannot change herself, or how she was with me as a mum.

Forgiveness is for you and not for the other person; it helps you make peace with what has occurred, with what you may not be able to reconcile, and helps you stop questioning what has taken place, and also stops you from focusing on the negative aspects and refocus on the positive.

It makes me sad that I didn't have a parental figure I could go to or rely on, however it does not benefit me to stay in that mindset; it is something I have to manage and come to terms with on a daily basis for my own wellbeing.

After watching my child struggle with their food aversions, and the way they walked, and a few other things I started to ask myself, "Am I autistic? Surely not." I did several online tests and they all said the same thing, yes. I also made an appointment (which unless you have access to funds is not accessible for everyone) and I got a formal diagnosis of also being Autistic.

The fact that I got the diagnosis just made so much sense of my life; the confusion, the not fitting in, the staring I've been accused of, being call weird and so much more; the social awkwardness and miscommunication.

I have only settled in one job, even got a promotion; but really struggled to settle into anything else after leaving that position, although I have always been able to obtain work.

I have emotional trauma from my beginnings and the way I was raised, and this also plays into my instability of employment, not always able to regulate or describe my emotions.

I have M.E. C.F.S, Inverse Psoriasis and Endometriosis. I am autistic so my poems encompass all these feelings. I have emotional issues, and due to the pandemic it has been hard for me to find a regular therapist to delve into this and to assist. I have severe anxiety and I recognise that I am an overthinker. I also think of the worst situation more than the best, and a lot of 'what ifs'. I have found my own way to come to terms with these issues, and poetry is one option that has helped.

Having M.E. CFS is like being hit by a bus, but being asked to get up one hour later to get on with life. The 'chronic fatigue' part of the name implicates just tiredness, but it is so much more than that: it's aches, cramps, headaches, insomnia, tiredness beyond exhaustion; but nothing visible to show that I am physically compromised.

Inverse Psoriasis is not just itchiness, it is a burning feeling, on some days relentless, unforgiving, pain and exhaustion, again causing sleep deprivation and requires ongoing management with creams, pain killers or whatever works on the day.

With my endometriosis, in the first years my cycle would last up to two weeks, which my teachers were concerned with and questioned; however, my mum was not the person to discuss these things with, and I'm not sure what they knew about Endometriosis back then either.

Due to my C.F.S I started to get more lower back pain and severe issues with my cycle. I initially ignored it but I did start asking questions. The event that brought this to a head was a skiing outing. Five of us went skiing and I felt alright even though I did have my cycle, but I had handled it before anyway I knew after one ski run something felt really bad. I asked my husband to check the chair and he said it was bad, so we skied straight to the bathrooms. I got new trousers and jocks and I was fine for the rest of the day.

When we got home, I called a clinic and talked about my issues, and they booked me in for a consultation and then a laparoscopy which I had in my mid-thirties. I was told my cycle would stop. It has not, and my Endometriosis has never totally gone away.

If I had hours and could articulate better, I could explain more about my autistic self. I have good hearing, yet I can have difficulty processing what you are saying, and will ask you to repeat yourself, most likely more than once. I am still awkward at social events, even with family, and I don't always react in the expected way, or say what I should. I am a contradictory; I like my alone/quiet time, but I do like to be with others. I can watch a movie over and over again if it appeals to me, or repeat a song a hundred times. These things give me comfort and certainty.

I see and understand things around me differently to others; I can be very literal which always gets a laugh.

I apologise for myself a lot. This is most likely a combination of everything above and I feel like I am always stepping on toes, in the way, or putting someone out.

I have been married for close to thirty years as I write this, and I cannot say enough about my husband. He did not get the best of me due to my C.F.S. diagnosis early in our marriage, and he was told by colleagues I was making it up to get out of house work. Are you serious? Who thinks like that and why would I make it up? He knew what I did and was capable of before the deterioration.

As much as he cannot understand what I have gone through with my parents, he has tried and he has always been there for me. It has not all been roses and I'm sure he would say I have not been an easy person, but he does not shy away from the difficult moments, he tries.

We have the same unique humour, the same thought processes, and unlike other people I can be direct with him, or I'll ask him to be clearer with his communication, and he won't be offended most of the time.

My husband encouraged me to start writing these poems as I was really struggling mentally and emotionally.

I have a few favourite places I like to visit and things I like to do, and when these things stopped being available, I had difficulty coping.

I struggle with compliments and kindness, and how to respond to any of those acts or words.

My two cats keep me entertained and amused. We adopted a greyhound that was cat tolerant, and she is an angel who gave me something else to think about and worry about, to feed and to walk, which assists in my mental health and focus on positive energy.

I know I missed my calling as they say. I am trying to complete a diploma, but due to the way my brain is wired it either happens quickly or not at all. I never found my full talent as I just did not have that support when I was younger, and I tried the university road but it's not for me.

For me to follow through, some part of me needs to be invested, excited, or engaged. If one or all of these things are missing then you've lost me and there's no bringing me back. That is probably why I only had one maths teacher that got the best out of me.

Not to mention I might be invested in something, but then find something else to take my interest and I will go in that direction, so it can be quite complicated. This is my brain; this is my life.

One of my children attempted suicide not long before the pandemic was declared. They were admitted to hospital immediately and we were fortunate that someone in their life was able to call emergency services and get them to a facility. They were put into an induced coma. It was very serious and we were not sure whether they were going to make it. We were by their side every day until and after they were woken up, then they were able to stay in a ward until fully recovered and were given a treatment plan. As a parent you feel helpless, and you ask yourself loads of questions, but you also know that this is out of your control. They are in a good place now and have an ongoing health plan.

My mum passed away Saturday 23rd of July at around 5:45pm surrounded by me, my sister, her eldest and two of my children. Mum's deterioration was quite quick, and accelerated due to the lockdowns and limitations on visits.

She would always smile when we walked in the room; I even brought my greyhound once for her to pat. She knew she was going to be a great grandmother for the second time.

Being able to accept and forgive goes a long way to assist me in managing my emotions. Your trauma does not need to be passed on to your children; it does not have to be a continued legacy.

For six days as soon as we all heard mum was in palliative care, she was surrounded by family until her last breath. She did not go down without a fight, which is one of the most true statements about my mum. She had suffered herself, going to an institution as a small child due to her mum going to prison for her siblings stealing food, then the car accident, a baby girl dying an hour after being born, spine and head trauma, two marriages both with their difficulties; and yet she still had a smile on her face. She was stubborn and a fighter even to her very last breath.

My employer has been very kind in these moments; however employers need to allow people time to readjust to loss in their lives, and it took me a while to feel normal again. I had to leave this position and go into another that was easier to manage by way of expectations and flexibility in taking time off.

It is OK to be upset, sad, conflicted when you have had difficult relationships, but in the end, it is how you deal with it, how you manage it that defines you as an individual. Do I regret not being there for my dad? Yes, and it will be an ongoing mental conflict, but I was younger and was still working myself out.

That is also the main reason I tried to find a way to accept what has been, that what has been cannot be changed, I just need to accept it; and this has helped me find peace within myself and those around me.

I cannot reiterate how proud I am of children, how they have supported me and other family members in this difficult time, and their love for my mum brings me a different type of joy and peace.

Final Goodbye

The grieving hasn't stopped
Tomorrow, we say goodbye
We lay you to rest
The week gone by has been in slow motion
We have had a glass of Moscato to celebrate you
The tears will stain our faces
Our hearts will be shattered into pieces of glass
No more will you be
You will be laid to rest
Our sadness will linger for a little longer
You have given all you can
A song will remind us of you
A smell will trigger a memory
Images will stay with us forever
It is time to let you go
Time to forge ahead
You have shaped us
We are linked for always
Never will you be forgotten.

Ode to My Children

In the moments that I called on you
You did not hesitate
You came in strong
You held me up
In those difficult moments you showed kindness
Thankfulness
Appreciated what has gone before and what is in front
Memories and stories treasured
Bore the burden of the darkest hours
Supported all in need
Shared stories
Embraced strength
I could not be prouder of you all
My children
Love Mum.